BALINESE
Temples

JULIAN DAVISON

& BRUCE GRANQUIST

PERIPLUS

Publisher: Eric M. Oey
Text: Julian Davison
Illustrations: Bruce Granquist, Mubinas Hanafi, Nengah Enu
Production: Mary Chia, Violet Wong & Agnes Tan

Distributors
Indonesia:
PT Wira Mandala Pustaka
(Java Books–Indonesia)
Jalan Kelapa Gading Kirana
Blok A14 No. 17
Jakarta 14240

Singapore and Malaysia:
Berkeley Books Pte. Ltd.
5 Little Road #08-01, Singapore 536983

United States:
Charles E. Tuttle Co., Inc.
RRI Box 231-5, North Clarendon
VT 05759-9700

Contents

Of Gods and Men

Unlike their Indian counterparts, Balinese shrines and sanctuaries do not generally include a physical representation of the deity to whom they are dedicated. There are, however, exceptions, as in the case of the Pura Penulisan, situated high on the crater walls surrounding Gunung Batur, where one finds this fine example of a stone *lingga* (below). In Hindu iconography, the *lingga* is a representation of the god Siwa, the phallic symbolism of the image being a celebration of the creative aspect of the deity. The veneration of the Hindu god Siwa plays an important role in Balinese religion, but *lingga* are usually found only in the oldest sanctuaries. Evidently the disappearance of a physical representation of the deity is something that happened after the introduction of Hinduism to Bali.

There are literally tens of thousands of temples and shrines on the island of Bali, a proliferation of religious architecture which probably is not equalled anywhere else in the world. Glimpsed through a screen of trees, or across a swathe of verdant rice fields, the Balinese temple seems almost to be a part of the natural order of things. Closer to hand, the crumbling brick work and lichen-covered statuary convey a sense of considerable antiquity, while the astonishing sculptural repertoire of demonic masks, multi-limbed deities and lurid depictions of sexuality that confront the Western eye, conjure up an exotic otherness of 'lost' civilisations and licentious natives—the 'Mysterious East' of all good Orientalist fantasies.

But Balinese temples need not be quite so mysterious if one takes an informed look at the underlying logic which determines the layout of the sanctuary and the symbolic significance of individual structures in the temple precincts.

Balinese Religion

The religion of Bali represents an eclectic blend of Hindu and Buddhist beliefs laid over a much older stratum of indigenous animism, and it is this combination of native and exotic influences which informs so much of Balinese life. The introduction of Indian religious beliefs to Southeast Asia began about the time of Christ and represents not so much a story of conquest and colonisation as one of cultural assimilation which followed in the wake of burgeoning trade links with the subcontinent. In the case of Bali, bronze edicts, written in Old Balinese, testify to the existence of an Indian-style court by the end of the 9th century, but Balinese Hinduism, as we know it today, owes more to East Javanese influences between the 14th and 16th centuries. The latter have subsequently been shaped by local traditions to create a singular form of Hinduism peculiar to the island.

Reincarnation and a Cosmic Order

Hinduism is founded on the assumption of a cosmic order which extends

to every aspect of the universe right down to the very smallest particle. This organising principle, or *dharma*, manifests itself in the persona of the gods, while demonic figures represent agents of disorder and chaos. As far as man is concerned he must try to conduct himself in a manner which is in keeping with his own personal *dharma*, the ultimate aim here being to gain liberation (*moksa*) from the endless cycle of reincarnation or rebirth to which he is otherwise destined. This objective can only be achieved by establishing a harmonious relationship with the rest of the universe, a beatific state which requires the subjugation of all worldly desires.

Microcosm and Macrocosm

Being in harmony with the rest of the universe requires, among other things, that one be correctly oriented in space. These ideas are represented, on the ground so to speak, in terms of local topographical features and the cardinal directions, which are attributed specific ritual and cosmological significations. In this respect, the island of Bali is con-

ceived as a replica of the universe in miniature—a microcosm of the macrocosm.

Central to this scheme of things, is the idea of a tripartite universe consisting of an underworld (*buhr*), inhabited by demons and malevolent spirits; the world of men (*buwah*); and the heavens (*swah*), where the gods and deified ancestors reside. In Bali, the mountains are conceived as the holiest part of the island while the sea is cast as a region of impurity and malign influences; mankind is sandwiched in between, tending to his rice fields and visiting his temples to pay his obeisances to the gods and placate the forces of evil.

A Tripartite Universe
The Balinese division of the universe (*tri loka*) into three domains—*buhr*, *buwah* and *swah*—dovetails with the concept of *tri angga* which posits that everything in the Balinese cosmos can be similarly divided into three components: *nista*, *madya* and *utama*. These categories are hierarchically ordered in terms of a set of spatial coordinates—high, middle and low—which in the case of human beings find a corporeal correspondence in a division of the body into three constituent parts—head, torso and feet. Buildings and other man-made objects can similarly be divided into three components. A simple column, for example, consists of a base, a shaft and a capital. This tripartite scheme of things ultimately extends to everything in the universe, from the Hindu trinity (*trimurti*) of Brahma, Siwa and Vishnu, to the works of man, including the temples that he builds, reflecting an essential unity underlying the whole of creation.

The Archetypal Temple

Although no two Balinese temples are exactly alike, they nevertheless conform to a basic pattern which is more or less the same in every part of the island. Things could not be otherwise for Balinese temples are laid out according to strict cosmological principles—to alter the basic design would be to admit to a change in the nature of the universe.

Correct Orientation in Space

The idea of ritual purity plays a crucial role in Balinese religion being identified as an essential requirement for a favourable reincarnation in the next life. Closely linked to the notion of a universal or cosmic order, it rests, in part, on the understanding that everything has its proper place in the world and that one must be correctly positioned in relation to the rest of the universe if one is to achieve a state of grace according to the principles of *dharma*.

Buildings are subject to the same rules of orientation and must be properly aligned if they are to serve the purpose they were designed for. As we have seen, in Bali, the mountains are the most holy of places, being identified as the abode of the gods, while the sea is represented as their antithesis, a place of impurity, the home of monstrous demons and other malevolent agencies. These ideas are defined locally by the terms *kaja* ('towards the mountains') and *kelod* ('towards the sea') and in southern Bali, where the majority of the island's population live, they correspond roughly with a north-south axis.

East (*kangin*) and west (*kauh*) are also important here, the east, where the sun rises, being identified with new life and other positive values, while the west, where it sets, is associated with death and decay. The point at which the sun reaches its zenith in the course of its daily passage makes up a third component in this scheme of things, which when combined with the *kaja-kelod* axis creates a nine-fold division of space based on the four cardinal directions, their four intermediaries, and the centre. This constitutes a kind of Balinese 'compass rose', the *nawa sanga*, where each point on the compass is identified with a particular deity in the Hindu pantheon and is ascribed a corresponding set of ritual or symbolic associations. In southern Bali, the northeast is conceived as the most auspicious, or sacred, direction, being a combination of 'towards the mountains' and 'east' (*kaja-kangin*).

Planning the Ideal Temple

The archetypal Balinese temple, or *pura*, consists of a series of three walled courtyards aligned on a linear axis running from the mountains to the sea. Ornamented gateways lead from one courtyard to the next and as one crosses each threshold one steps up a level.

In symbolic terms, the temple complex constitutes a spatial metaphor for the Hindu cosmos, the three courtyards replicating the tripartite nature of the universe with each ascending level representing a higher state of purity or sacredness.

The outermost courtyard, or *jaba*, serves a kind of reception area where

Mount Meru

The idea of mountains as holy places, and more specifically as the abode of the gods, finds a natural accord with Indian mythology where the deities are portrayed as living in caves on the slopes of a sacred mountain—Mount Meru or Mahameru—which is situated at the centre of the universe. In Bali, this legendary mountain is generally identified with Gunung Agung, at 3,014 metres, the highest peak on the island. Architecturally, Mount Meru is represented by a tower-like edifice of the same name. The latter are wooden structures, standing on a masonry base, surmounted by a series of stepped roofs, placed one on top of another which give them a general appearance not unlike that of a Chinese pagoda. Interestingly, the idea of a sacred mountain would also seem to be part of a much older cultural tradition in the region: pre-historic stone terraces, cut into the sides of prominent peaks, have been found in many parts of the Indonesian archipelago, including Bali, testifying to a very ancient veneration for high places.

Temple layout

1. *Bale kulku, or* drum tower.
2. *Bale gong*–pavilion for *gamelan* performances.
3. *Gedong sinub westra*–for storing ritual paraphernalia.
4. *Peranteng*–kitchen for the preparation of food and offerings.
5. *Piasan pedanda*–pavilion reserved for priests
6. *Apit lawang*–paired shrines flanking the gateways leading into each of the courtyards, where offerings are placed for the guardians of the temple precincts.
7. *Pesantian*–pavilion for performing ritual invocations.
8. *Piasan dauh*–pavilion for storing ritual paraphernalia.
9. *Piasan ratu gede*–pavilion for ritual paraphernalia.
10. *Pelinggih gedong*–pavilion dedicated to temple founder.
11. *Padmasana*–shrine dedicated to the supreme godhead and prime mover of the Universe, Ida Sanghyang Widhi Wasa.
12. *Pewedaan betara*–where the gods receive the prayer of the priests.
13. *Pewedaan pemangku*–pavilion where lay priests offer their prayers.
14. *Peselang*–pavilion for holding small-scale rituals.

people gather at festival times to eat and socialise, while the middle courtyard, or *jaba tenga*, represents a transitional space between the secular world of men and the sacred domain of the gods. The latter is constituted by the innermost courtyard or *jeroan*, which stands at the *kaja* end of the temple complex and is oriented towards the mountains from which, it is hoped, the gods will descend during temple ceremonies. This is where the most important shrines and ritual structures are located and where the gods are seated during temple festivals.

Other structures within the temple precincts include open-sided pavilions which provide protection for the priests when they are performing their ritual duties and constitute a work space when the community is preparing for a temple ceremony. One pavilion will be reserved as a place for the *gamelan* orchestra to perform.

The *padmasana* is in effect a representation of the cosmos in miniature. The base is divided vertically into three stepped platforms corresponding to the three principle divisions of the cosmos—*buhr* (the netherworld of the demons), *buwah* (the realm of man) and *swah* (the domain of the gods). A stone throne sits on top with a high back which often is ornamented with a carving of a swan or alternatively an eagle, the swan being the identified as the mount, or vehicle, of Brahma, and the eagle, that of Vishnu.

A Resting Place for the Gods

Balinese temples are not conceived as places where the gods are permanently in residence, but rather as temporary sanctuaries where the gods alight when they descend from the heavens to attend a temple ceremony.

Unlike Hindu temples in India and in ancient Java, there are no physical representations of the deities housed in the various pavilions and shrines that provide a sanctuary for the gods during Balinese temple festivals. The gods are, however, invited to inhabit small wooden effigies called *pratima*. The latter come in pairs, the larger, more animal-like, of the two representing the mount upon which the deity rides.

The most important ritual structures are situated in the inner sanctum, or *jeroan*, but there are places for offerings located at other strategic points in the temple complex— for example, on either side of the principal gateways which lead from one courtyard to another. Gateways themselves play an important part in

the symbolic order of Balinese temple architecture, creating thresholds between the secular world outside and the realm of the sacred within.

Padmasana

There are two principal types of shrine—the *padmasana*, or 'lotus seat', and the *meru*, a wooden house-like structure with a masonry base and a multi-tiered roof. The *padmasana* is a small stone seat, raised some one and a half metres off the ground, and is intended as a resting place for the gods when they attend a temple festival.

There are three basic types which are classified according to the number of seats provided. The single-seater version is identified as the throne of Siwa, or alternatively, the sun-god Surya. Then there is a double-seated version which is dedicated to the deified ancestors—one male and one female. Finally there is a triple-seated version which may also be dedicated to the ancestors, or alternatively to the Hindu trinity (*trimurti*) of

Candi Bentar

The *candi bentar*, or split gateway, is a distinctive feature of Balinese temple architecture. They typically stand at the main entrance to a temple or on the threshold of the outer and middle courtyards where they mark a transition from the secular world to the sacred domain of the inner precincts. In elevation the *candi bentar* characteristically has a stepped profile, which is lavishly decorated with carvings and reliefs, though the two inner surfaces, as one passes through the portal, are left sheer and unornamented. The architectural origins of *candi bentar* date back to the days of the Majapahit Empire in Java (1292-c.1520), though the symbolism of this bifurcated gateway remains uncertain. The Mexican artist and writer Miguel Covarrubias, who lived in Bali during the 1930s, records a Balinese explanation, namely that the *candi bentar* represents the legendary Mount Meru of Hindu mythology which was split in two by Pasupati (Siwa) and placed in Bali as the twinpeaks of Gunung Agung and Gunung Batur.

Peppelik or panuman,

The *peppelik* or *panuman,* is located at the centre of the inner sanctum and serves as the communal seat of the gods when they descend from the heavens on the ocasion of a festival. There are also miniature houses for Ngrurah Alit and Ngrurah Gede, the secretaries of the gods, who make sure that the appropriate offerings are made, and a stone niche is reserved for the Taksú, or interpreter of the gods. The latter enters the body of mediums during trance and through them makes known the decisions of the deities.

Construction Rites

Miniature iron implements are buried beneath the shrine, together with small quantities of gold and silver, lotus flowers, crabs, prawns and a roast chicken. Where the rafters of the uppermost roof meet, there is a vertical column with a cavity into which is placed a small bowl containing either nine precious stones or else nine *pripih.* The latter are thin plates of various metals which are inscribed with cabalistic words. Excavations in Java reveal similar ritual practices were employed in the construction of the great Hindu-Buddhist temples of Indonesia's Classical era.

Brahma, Siwa and Vishnu. The most important *padmasana* is placed in the most sacred (*kaja-kangin*) corner of the inner courtyard with its back to Gunung Agung. This shrine is dedicated to the Supreme Deity, Ida Sanghaya Widhi Wasa in his manifestation as Siwa Raditya, the Balinese counterpart of the ancient Hindu sun-god, Surya.

Meru

As its name suggests, the *meru* symbolises the legendary Mount Meru of Indian mythology which is identified as the abode of the gods. Individual *meru* will either be dedicated to specific gods in the Balinese Hindu pantheon, or a deified ancestor, or else the deity of a particular location or geographical feature, such as a mountain or lake. *Meru* are constructed from wood and are raised on stilts, like miniature houses. They stand on a masonry base and are surmounted by a series of thatched roofs of diminishing size. The number of roofs is always odd and reflects the status of the deity to whom the shrine is dedicated, the most prestigious being accorded 11 tiers.

Meru are regularly erected in honour of the deities associated with the island's two highest peaks,

Gunung Agung and Gunung Batur, — Ida Bhatara Gunung Agung qualifies for a *meru* with an 11-storey roof.

Images of the legendary white monkey, Hanuman, are common in the Balinese iconographic repertoire. Hanuman features prominently in the *Ramayana*, as the general of the monkey army which helped Rama and Laksamana recapture the former's wife, Sati, from the devilish Rawana, King of Sri Lanka, who had abducted her.

Bhoma head from Desa Pakudi, Gianyar. The image is clearly related to the *kala* heads that are found over the doorways of Javanese temples dating from the Classical era of Indonesia's Hindu-Buddhist past.

Ornamentation and Iconography

Balinese temples are enlivened by a variety of stone sculptures and reliefs which to the Western eye have an almost baroque or rococo quality. The original inspiration for many of the statues and motifs may have come from India, but everywhere they have been subjected to strong local influences which over centuries have given rise to a uniquely Balinese artistic tradition.

The basic material used for stone carving is a soft volcanic sandstone, or tuff, which has a very plastic quality and lends itself well to being shaped by the stone mason's chisel. Equally, it deteriorates fairly rapidly when exposed to the elements and Balinese temples are in a constant process of renovation and renewal.

A Balinese Iconography

One of the most striking images in Balinese temples is the face of a leering monster, with lolling tongue, bulging eyes and ferociously large canines, which is typically found over the monumental gateway (*kori agung*) leading to the innermost courtyard. This demonic visage is the face of the *bhoma*, whose fearful countenance is intended to drive away malevolent influences from the temple precincts.

Less important locations are augmented with *karang bintulu*—a monstrous single eye which stares unblinkingly over a dental arcade of upper teeth with extended canines. This motif is typically surmounted by an image of a mountain—a representation of the legendary Mount Meru which stands at the centre of the Hindu-Buddhist universe and is identified in Indian mythology as the abode of the gods.

Corner motifs include *karang curing*, which are composed by the upper part of a bird's beak with a single eye and jagged teeth, or as an alternative, *karang asti*, the jawless head of an elephant. When the Mexican artist and author Miguel Covarrubias, who lived in Bali during the 1930s, asked why these images lacked a lower mandible, he was told that this was because they did not have to eat solid food. Covarrubias comments: "This is, in my opinion, a typical Balinese wisecrack and not an indication of any such symbolic meaning"

Other decorative motifs include border designs (*patra*) of which there are several kinds. The type known as *patra olanda* might have been inspired by Dutch sources, while the pattern known as *patra cina*, indicates Chinese origins.

Padmasana shrines and *meru* are typically decorated with geometric or foliate motifs, while the carvings on pavilions may include representations of animals and mythological beasts, or even the gods themselves.

The most important images are reserved for the walls and gateways for they divide the sacred precincts of the temple from the profane, secular world outside. Especially significant in this last respect are the reliefs which adorn the free-standing wall, or *aling aling*, which is placed just behind the *kori agung* gateway as one enters the innermost courtyard in the temple complex. The latter typically sports a rogues' gallery of demons and ogres who are intended to deter malevolent influences from penetrating the inner sanctum.

(above) Wall carving from Taman Pura Puleh, Mas.

(left) Typical foliate decorative element, Desa Sebatu, Gianyar.

(right) Highly decorated shrine from the compound of a priestly (Brahmin) family. The carved woodwork is highlighted with gold leaf.

Heroes and Villains

Temple reliefs frequently depict well-known scenes or episodes from Indian Classical literature. The *Ramayana* and *Mahabarata* epics provide a rich source of inspiration, but other favourites include erotic encounters from the *Arjuna Wiwaha* which portray luscious nymphs making passionate love to the god Arjuna, and charming vignettes from the *tantri* tales, the Balinese equivalent of Aesop's fables. Often there is humorous element to these representations—Covarrubias likens the reliefs in north Bali to American-style comic strips. A well-known example at the Pura Dalem, Jagaraga, a little to the east of Singaraja, shows a car driven by bearded foreigners being held up by a gangster armed with a revolver, while at the nearby Pura Meduwe Karang, in Kubutambahan, there is an image of a European man, riding a bicycle with a lotus flower for a rear wheel. The latter is said to be a portrait of the Dutch artist W.O.J. Nieuwenkamp, who visited Bali in the early years of this century.

Relief depicting a scene from the *Ramayana*, Desa Kabakaba, Tabanan. Rama and Laksamana are in the top right-hand corne, while Hanuman and members of his monkey army approach from the leftt.

Comic relief from Sibang Gede, Tabanan: a mischievous monkey catches a chicken by the foot.

Taman Ayun

Taman Ayun is notable for its majestic *kori agung* gateway and soaring *meru* towers which are dedicated to the gods who dwell on high, atop the lofty peaks of Gunung Batukaru, Pengelegan, Batur and Agung. The temple was built in honour of the ancestors of the royal family of Mengwi and at the *kaja* end of the inner sanctum there is a brick structure—a *paibon* or offering place—which together with three brick *prasada* nearby, is dedicated to these deified predecessors (the base of the *paibon* is remarkable for its bifurcated *bhoma* head). The temple complex is surrounded by a moat, filled with water, and was built as an earthly replica of the heavens where the deified ancestors disport themselves in floating pavilions attended to by celestial nymphs. This idea of creating a heavenly garden here on earth was quite common in Java during the Classical era. Other Balinese examples include the royal palace at Klungkung and Taman Ujung in the former Kingdom of Karangasem.

A Typology of Temples

A conservative estimate reckons that there are some 20,000 temples in Bali. Most of the time they are deserted, watched over by a lay priest, or *pemangku,* who keeps the temple precincts clear of leaves and acts as a general caretaker. But every temple has its birthday festival, or *odalan,* whose date is fixed either according to a 210-day ritual cycle, or alternatively the ancient Hindu lunar Saka calendar. An *odalan* may last for several days, and their principal aim is the ritual purification of the temple catchment area and its congregation. On these occasions, the temple becomes the centre of intense activity drawing in the entire local community to participate in prayer and ritual supplication to the gods and to partake of the associated entertainments—*gamelan* performances, puppet theatre, dance-drama, operetta and the like.

Temples for All Occasions

There are a great variety of temple types in Bali, each serving a different function. Every village, or *desa,* has three main temples which govern the religious life of the community. They are known as the *kahyangan tiga* and they are identified with the Hindu trinity of Brahma, Vishnu and Siwa. Other kinds of temples include *pura panataran,* or royal temples, which are usually incorporated as part of a palace complex, and private origin temples dedicated to the ancestors of a particular family— variously *pura dadia, pura kawitan* and *pura padharman,* depending on the genealogical depth being traced. There are also hill temples (*pura bukit*), sea temples (*pura segara*) and temples dedicated to the tutelary gods of seed (*pura melanting*) and markets (*pura pasar*). Each irrigation society—a collective of rice farmers who draw their water from a common source—will also have its own temple (*ulun carik*).

Sad Kahyangan

Especially prominent temples in the religious life of Bali are the 'six great sanctuaries', or 'temples of the world' (*sad kahyangan*) which are recognised as the most sacred sites on the island. They include Pura

Luhur Uluwatu at the westernmost tip of the Bukit Peninsula, Pura Goa Lawah near Kusamba, Pura Lempuyang Luhur in Karangasem, Pura Batukau in Tabanan and Pura Pusering Jagat in Pejeng. The most sacred temple of all is Pura Besakih, on the southern slopes of Gunung Agung, which is identified as the 'mother temple' of all Bali. Other important regional temples include the 'temples of the Sacred Ones'—*pura dang kahyangan*—which are associated with the legendary Javanese priests who brought Hinduism to Bali.

King and Cosmos

In traditional Hindu cosmology, the political territory of a kingdom is conceived, in symbolic terms, as being coterminous with the universe as a whole, a microcosm of the macrocosm. In this respect, the seat of the ruler, which was ideally situated at, or near, the geographical centre of the kingdom, was perceived not only as the ultimate source of temporal power but also as a cosmological and ritual centre. The two aspects of power went hand in hand, the ruler, in Classical Indonesia, being regarded as divinely appointed (*cakravartin*).

The Kingdom of Mengwi

The temple of Pura Taman Ayun was once the state temple of the kingdom of Mengwi which flourished in the 17th and 18th centuries. The actual sanctuary itself was founded in the mid-18th century and reflects an attempt to literally re-centre the kingdom following a power struggle between rival factions within the royal family. The ascendant house decided to consolidate its advantage by building a new temple complex at Taman Ayun, situated halfway along a line running between Gunung Pengelengan—the local Mount Olympus—and the coastal temple of Pura Ulun Siwi. In cosmological terms this point was identified as the 'navel' (*puseh*) of the world, an *axis mundi* situated midway between the heavens and the Stygian seas.

Celestial figures inhabit every possible nook and cranny, including the bases of pillars–this one comes from the *kaja*-most *meru*.

The *panuman* in the inner courtyard of Taman Ayun, provides a pavilion for the gods when they descend from the mountain tops to attend a festival.

Village Temples

Balinese society is complex and multi-farious, being divided by social hierar-chies based on caste, occupation and descent. In the not so distant past, the life of the ordinary man, or common-er, was largely restricted to his village and its surrounding rice fields, while at a supra-village level there existed an upper crust of priests, noblemen and princes, organised into a ruling elite. These divisions are still in evi-dence today—though the plight of the common man is far less onerous—but they are mediated by the village tem-ple system and the cycle of festivals associated with them, which periodi-cally draw these diverse groups together as common participants in a shared ritual undertaking.

The Balinese Village

The Balinese village is referred to by the term *desa*, which describes both the settlement and its immediate

Kahyangan Tiga

Balinese villages, like Balinese temples, are typically arranged along a linear axis running between the mountains and the sea. Each village has three main places of worship, the *kahyangan tiga*, which service the religious needs of the community. This system of three village temples is said to have been initiated by Mpu Kuturan, the legendary Javanese priest who was responsible for a reformation of Balinese Hinduism during the 11th century.

The *pura puseh*, or temple of origin, which is dedicated to the communi-ty founders, is situated at the uphill, or *kaja* end of the village, as befits the rarefied status of the village ancestors, while the cemetery and temple of dead, *pura dalem*, are located at the downhill, or seaward, *kelod* end, usu-ally a little outside the village, reflecting the ritual pollution of death. The principal village temple, the *pura desa*, which constitutes the ritual and social focal point of the community, is typically situated at the very heart of the settlement—either in the village square or on a prominent crossroads.

Kaja

1. Pura Puseh
2. Pura Desa
3. Pura Dalem

environs as a physical entity, and at the same time refers to a religious community, made up of local householders and their families, who are responsible for maintaining the ritual purity and spiritual well-being of the village and its surrounding lands. The latter is achieved by observing the local customary laws (*desa adat*) and by participation in the cycle of religious ceremonies that take place at the village temples.

The actual village itself, as a collection of house compounds, is subdivided into neighbourhoods, or wards (*banjar*), each of which have their own local temple *(pura pamaskan)*. Every *banjar* has specific ritual duties to fulfill, not only in relation to its own neighbourhood temple, but also to the main village temples. *Banjar* members also act together in secular matters such as the maintenance of roads and the policing of the neighbourhood.

Pura Desa

Pura desa are ideally placed in an auspicious location at the centre of the village—a position which is both towards the mountains (*kaja*) and to the east (*kangin*). A sacred banyan tree is usually planted beside the entrance which often grows to enormous proportions, providing a shady centre at the heart of the community. A pavilion (*wantilan*) for cockfights is also located nearby—the sacrificial shedding of blood (*caru*) plays a crucial role in Balinese rituals and contests are permitted on the occasion of a temple festival, though gambling is strictly prohibited, in theory at least, by the Indonesian government.

Village assemblies to discuss both ritual and secular matters are held every month, either at the *pura desa* itself or else at the village assembly hall (*bale agung*) nearby. One of the principal responsibilities of the village assembly is the organisation of the anniversary celebrations (*odalan*) for each of the village temples. The latter fall every 210 days, according to the sacred *wuku* calendar, and are intended to ritually cleanse the village territory and purify the members of the temple congregation. Everyone in the village is involved in the preparation of offerings and the organisation of various entertainments such as *gamelan* recitals and shadow puppet performances which are held for the enjoyment of the gods and mortals alike.

Pura Desa Batuan
The main entrance to Pura Desa Batuan. Batuan has for centuries been famous as both a religious and artistic centre and the aesthetic achievements of local craftsmen are well in evidence at the *pura desa* which underwent major restoration work in 1992.

Bale Kulkul
The *bale kulkul* is a tower-like structure found in most Balinese temples, and houses a large wooden drum or *kulkul*, which is used as a summons to village assemblies or to sound the alarm in times of danger.

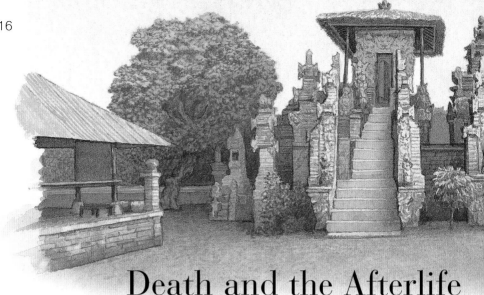

Death and the Afterlife

The *pura dalem* at Jaga Raga, a little to the east of the port of Singaraja.

A statue of Rangda from the Pura Dalem, Gunung Salak, Tabanan. This demonic witch-like creature, with her tangled hair, lolling tongue and pendulous breasts, is identified as an agent of death and destruction—the word *rangda* in high Balinese means 'widow'.

Death in Bali is considered to be both ritually polluting and contaminating. These perceptions are reflected in the location of the *pura dalem*—the community temple where funerary rites are held—at the inauspicious, seaward end (*kelod*) of the village and also a little to the west, the setting sun in Bali being identified with the passing of life. The community graveyard and cremation site are located nearby—the cremation ground is usually simply a clearing in the cemetery at the most *kelod* end.

Pura dalem can often be spotted from some distance away by the presence of *kapok* trees (*Ceiba pentandra*), with their distinctive horizontal branches and cotton bearing pods, which are frequently planted in the vicinity.

Siwa, Durga and Rangda

Hindu deities are typically perceived as having a number of different attributes or guises and *pura dalem* are usually dedicated to Siwa in his destructive aspect, though Siwa is of course also conceived as a god of creative energies. This apparent conflict of interests between these dual

natures is not so much a case of contradiction as one of complementarity, for death, in the Hindu scheme of things, is merely one stage in an endless cycle of reincarnation and in this last respect, it is a necessary prelude to rebirth.

The creative aspect of Siwa is often personified in his wife, Durga, but she too, like her husband, has a dark, destructive side to her, metamorphosing into the demonic witch-like Rangda, whom the anthropologist Clifford Geertz describes as a "monstrous queen of the witches, ancient widow, used-up prostitute, child-murdering incarnation of the goddess of death".

Death and the Fate of the Soul

There are a number of perspectives on the post-mortem fate of the soul in Bali. Some are mutually exclusive and would logically deny all other possibilities; others are more tolerant of rival interpretations. Two explanations, however, would seem to prevail in Balinese accounts of what happens to the soul after death.

The first of these supposes that the correct performance of mortuary rituals, including cremation, ensures

that the soul, which at the moment of death is impure, will subsequently be purified, thus enabling it to merge with a collective ancestral deity. The Balinese are rather vague about the precise nature of this aggregate ancestral spirit, but it is sometimes said to be responsible for the spiritual welfare and general health and well-being of living descendants.

The second point of view assumes that the soul of the deceased is subject to divine judgment based on the relative merit, or moral discredit, of deeds carried out during the dead person's life time. Depending on the final 'score', which is reckoned according to the laws of *karma-pala* (literally, 'actions' and their 'fruit'), the soul is then sentenced to a period in the afterworld—either Heaven or Hell as the case may be—before being reborn into the world of the living again.

Burial and Cremation

The pollution of death is reflected not only in the *kelod* location of the graveyard, but also in the degradation of being interred underground.

Should there be sufficient funds, an immediate cremation is preferred since this skips the burial stage. In the case of members of a royal family, it is considered unseemly that such an illustrious corpse should be placed in the ground, so the body is preserved, lying in state, in a special pavilion in the palace compound, until suitable preparations for a lavish cremation ceremony have been completed and there is an auspicious day in the Balinese calendar for the ceremony to take place. This lying in state period may last for months, even years. Priests are not buried either, there being a ritual prohibition on their interment.

Cremation (*ngaben*) releases the soul from its ties to the earth, returning the five elemental constituents of the body—earth, fire, water, air and space—to the cosmos. The ashes are thrown in a river or cast upon the sea, with the final mortuary rites being held some 12 days later (longer in the case of the *triwangsa* castes). These complete the Balinese cycle of death rituals, at which point the newly-purified soul becomes incorporated with those of the ancestors.

A Balinese Hades

Those who have led a less than meritorious life, must face divine retribution in the next. The Balinese Hell (Neraka) is located in the subterranean world (*bhur*) of demons and malevolent spirits, and it is to this frightful place that the souls of the wicked are consigned after their demise. Their punishment depends on the kinds of misdemeanour they have committed during their lifetime and the post-mortem fate of those found guilty of evil misdoings are graphically portrayed in the temple reliefs at *pura dalem*. The consequences of fornication and sexual misconduct are often an excuse to introduce an erotic or ribald element into these images which can be a source of amusement and titillation for both Balinese and tourist alike.

A relief depicting a drowning sailor being consumed by sea monsters, from the Pura Dalem at Jaga Raga.

Sacred Rice and Subak Temples

Sacred Rice

Rice has been cultivated in Asia for several thousands of years and everywhere that it is grown it is surrounded by ritual pre-scriptions and prohibitions. Rice is commonly assumed to have a soul, whose presence, or absence, determines the success (or failure) of the harvest. Often the increase of rice is symbolically identified with the fertility of women—in Bali, the ripening rice plants are said to be 'pregnant' (*beling*) while the principal rice deity is the goddess Dewi Sri, who is the perfect realisation of feminine grace and charm.

Rice and its cultivation are central to the Balinese way of life. In Balinese eyes, rice is a gift from the gods—it was created by the Hindu deity Vishnu who then presented it to man as his divine patrimony. In this respect, rice is a sacred thing whose cultivation entails not only planting and looking after the crop as it grows towards maturity, but also requires the careful implementation of a set of ritual procedures first laid down by the god Indra.

Subak Associations

The modern Balinese farmer grows two crops of rice each year in irrigated, terraced rice fields which for many are the definitive feature of the Balinese landscape. Water sources in the mountains are directed to each individual rice field by an intricate network of channels and aqueducts, whose maintenance and regulation are governed by local cooperative organisations called *subak*. Each mini-watershed has its own *subak* council, made up from neighbouring farmers who are party to this common water supply: together they are responsible for the equable distribution of water to all the irrigated rice fields within their purview.

Each *subak* council has its own temple (*ulun carik*), which is situated in the middle of the rice fields belonging to its members, and this is where the major ceremonies of the rice cycle are held. The temple of Ulun Danau, on Lake Bratan, is identified as the 'mother' temple of all the *subak* systems on the island and some *subak* associations make regular pilgrimages to this sanctuary immediately prior to irrigating their rice fields. There are also countless small, roofless shrines (*bedugul*), which are commonly found in cultivated areas, typically beside a dam or weir. These tend to be erected and maintained by individual farmers whose rice fields are in the vicinity.

A Balinese Harvest Home

The most important *subak* ceremony in the agricultural cycle is the festival of *ngusaba nini*, which is usually held either just before or immediately after the rice harvest. It is held at the *subak* association temple and takes the form of a thanksgiving ceremony dedicated to the rice goddess Dewi Sri. Dewi Sri is the wife of Vishnu and is one of the most popular deities in the Balinese pantheon, being conceived as the paragon of everything that is good and beautiful. Furthermore, as rice goddesss, she is identified as the fountainhead of agricultural fertility and bountiful harvests, while

her daughter, Dewi Melanting, is the tutelary deity of seed and plants.

For the rites of *ngusaba nini*, a mouth-watering selection of offerings are prepared by *subak* association members, and after they have been dedicated by the priests to the beneficent gods, and in particular to Dewi Sri, they are shared amongst the participants at the festival. As with all temple offerings, the gods are said to enjoy the essence (*sari*) of whatever is presented to them, leaving its material residue for the delectation of their followers.

Pura Ulun Danau Bratan

Pura Ulun Danau Bratan was built by the ruler of Mengwi in 1633 and consists of four compounds, two of which are detached from the main temple complex on little islets a few metres from the shore. A bubbling spring, together with a large white stone flanked by two red ones–a phallic *lingga* no less–were uncovered during restoration of the three-tiered *meru* on one of the islets, indicating a Sivaite connection. The main *meru* with the 11-tiered roof on the neighbouring islet is dedicated to Vishnu in his manifestation as the lake goddess Dewi Danu, the saviour of all living creatures. As well as being the creator of rice and the husband of the goddess Sri, Vishnu is also responsible for regulating the flow of terrestrial waters, hence his association with *subak* temples.

The main pavilion, or *gedong,* at Pura Ulun Danau Bratan, decked out for a temple ceremony.

Gunung Kawi
Sometimes called the 'Royal Tombs', these deeply cut reliefs at Gunung Kawi may commemorate the 11th-century Balinese king, Anak Wungsu.

Goa Gajah
The remarkable facade of the Goa Gajah cave temple has been sculpted directly from the rock face. It features monstrous creatures and the leering face of demonic being whose mouth forms the entrance portal. No doubt the latter was intended to prevent malevolent influences from entering the sanctuary.

Cave Temples and Rock-cut Sanctuaries

The practice of carving temples out of solid rock has an ancient history in India dating back to the time of the great Mauryan emperor Ashoka (c. 270-232 BC). Some of the earliest surviving sanctuaries in Bali have also been hewn from a rock face, the best known of these being Gunung Kawi and Goa Gajah. They are both to be found in the vicinity of Gianyar, in the narrow strip of land lying between the Petanu and Pakrisan rivers, a region which is extraordinarily rich in ancient temple sites and sanctuaries.

Gunung Kawi
Gunung Kawi, which literally means 'Mountain of the Poet(s)', consists of a series of temple-like 'structures', standing in two rows of niches, excavated directly from the rock face. Though no more than deeply-cut reliefs, in form they resemble Classical Javanese temples, or *candi*, with their stepped pyramidal roofs and serried ranks of antefixes, but the 'doors' do not open and there are no internal spaces.

Nevertheless they are commemorative structures, with inscriptions over the false doorways indicating to whom they are dedicated. The latter are executed in a highly decorative script, sometimes known 'Kadiri Quadrate' after the East Javanese kingdom of Kadiri where it is also

found in the late 10th and 11th centuries. Unfortunately, these inscriptions are badly worn and are virtually illegible except in the case of one associated with the central *candi* which reads "*haji lumah ing Jalu*" (literally, "the king who was 'monumentalised' at Jalu"). The king referred to here is generally thought to be the 11th-century Balinese ruler, Anak Wungsu. Known chiefly from royal proclamations carved in stone, Anak Wungsu probably ruled from about 1050 until at least 1078 (the date of his last inscription).

Sacred Serpents and Fecundity

There is a conduit on the hillside above the group of five rock-cut *candi* which carries water to a lower channel that passes right in front of the *candi* themselves. There are spouts in front of each of the *candi* and water issues forth from these into another conduit which empties

into a bathing place. The spout in front of the central *candi*, commemorating the deceased king, is carved in the shape of a *naga* serpent (the other spouts are plain). *Naga* are traditionally associated with water and fertility throughout Southeast Asia and it seems likely that in the past it was believed that immersion in water which had come into contact with the memorial to the late ruler would enhance fecundity or cure barrenness and other ills.

Cloisters and Meditation Cells

The so-called 'cloisters' (*patapan*) at Gunung Kawi consist of a series of courtyards, monks' cells and meditation niches, which again have all been cut from the rock face. The largest of these chambers has windows and a hole in the ceiling to admit light. There is a central dais and stone seats let into the surrounding walls, rather like a chapter house in a medieval monastery in Europe.

Telaga Waja

Telaga Waja, on the Tukad Kungkang river, consists of two pools, one of which is slightly higher than the other. They are both filled by a spring located above the river. Three niches are cut into the hillside next to the upper pool and there is a small temple courtyard, on a raised terrace, to the south of the lower one, which is also surrounded by niches. The latter were probably used as places of meditation.

Sacred Bathing Places

Water has a special place in Balinese life, not only because of the vital role it plays in irrigating the island's rice fields, but also because of its ritual significance as an agent of purification. With its source in the volcanic lakes and rushing streams of the central mountain range, water is identified with the purity of the gods who dwell on high. Eventually, however, it flows to the sea where it enters the realm of greatest impurity. And along the way it picks up the dirt of man, both in the literal sense—the Balinese are very conscious of personal cleanliness and bathe themselves in running water several times a day—and also in terms of spiritual pollution. It is in this last respect that water acts as a purifying agent, cleansing man of his mortal sins and preparing his soul for a better reincarnation in the next life.

Holy Water

Holy water (*tirtha*) is the key ingredient in this scheme of things, being the principal means by which various forms of impurity are ritually washed down to the sea. The preparation of holy water is a sacrament of great importance in Balinese religion which the Balinese themselves often refer to as the *agma tirtha,* or 'holy water religion'. The degree of potency of holy water is contingent on its source, the status of the person who prepares it, and the type of mantra employed in its preparation. The holiest of holy waters comes from high up in the mountains and is prepared by high-status Brahmana priests (*pedanda*).

Sacred Bathing Places

Every village has a recognised bathing place—either the nearby river or a community bath, with sep-

Tirtha Empul

The baths at Tirtha Empul are perhaps the most ancient and holy of Bali's sacred bathing places. A stone inscription at the nearby temple of Pura Sakenan, in the village of Manukaya, mentions the place name 'Tirtha de [air] mpul' and this is assumed to be a reference to the Tirtha Empul pools. The inscription records that they were built by one Sang ratu (Sri) Candra Bhaya Singha Varmadeva, in the district of the village of Manuk Raya (present-day Manukaya) in the year 882 according to the Saka era calendar, that is to say around AD 960. Local legend, however, provides a more romantic account of their origin, attributing the baths to the god Indra who summoned forth the spring which feeds them during a military campaign to overthrow the evil and despotic Balinese prince, Mayadenawa.

This version relates how one night, when Indra's troops were sleeping, Mayadenawa crept into their camp and using his occult powers, conjured up a poison spring. The next day, Indra's men awoke and drank from the contaminated water which caused them to become violently ill. Fortunately Indra realised what had happened and immediately created a new spring from which gushed forth holy water, restoring his army to health. Since then, the place has been known as Tirtha Empul, *tirtha* being the term for holy water and *empul* the word for a 'big spring' in Old Javanese.

arate compartments for men and women to perform their ablutions. In addition, there are numerous sacred pools and bathing places whose waters are deemed to have magical or curative qualities. The central Balinese regency of Gianyar is particularly well-endowed with sacred bathing sites. The best known of these are Tirtha Empul, near the village of Tampaksiring, Pura Mengening, a little to the south, Telaga Waja and Goa Gajah, but there are several other sacred bathing places in the vicinity of the Sungai Petanu and Pakerisan rivers which flow through Gianyar from the mountains in the north to the waters of the Straits of Badung in the south.

Goa Gajah

The baths at Goa Gajah consist of two main pools with a smaller one in between. The two larger baths were probably intended for men and women to bathe in separately and were fed by water which gushed forth from spouts in the shape of heavenly nymphs or *apsara*.

The Majapahit Past

The *kori agung* gateway of Pura Maospahit, in the district of Gerenceng, Denpasar, is built in the Majapahit style and It is just possible that some of the earliest parts of the temple complex may date back to that era. The name Maospahit, which is clearly a variant of Majapahit, is also the name of a Balinese deity, Batara Maospahit, who is credited with having introduced Majapahit culture to the island.

The temples of Bali are the legacy, in part, of an architectural tradition that dates back to the last great empire of Indonesia's Hindu-Buddhist past, namely the East Javanese kingdom of Majapahit, which at the height of its influence between the 14th and 15th centuries held sway over most of the Indonesian archipelago.

Construction techniques employed by the ancient Javanese are still used today in Bali and many architectural elements—most notably the distinctive split gateway, or *candi bentar*—can be traced back to the golden Majapahit era.

Majapahit and Bali

Bali first came under the hegemony of Java in the latter part of the 13th century when the last ruler of Singasari, the dynasty which preceded Majapahit in East Java, sent a military expedition to subjugate the island in 1284. The subsequent fall of Singasari in 1292 temporarily released Bali from the thrall of East Java, but early in the 14th century, the new Majapahit rulers conducted a series of military campaigns against Bali which culminated in the installation of a Javanese king at Samprangan and the establishment of a Javanese ruling elite across the island.

The end of the 15th century saw a gradual decline in Majapahit fortunes as autonomous Muslim entrepôt states began to establish themselves along the northern coastline of Java. The final collapse of Majapahit came at the beginning of the 16th century and led to a huge influx of Javanese refugees into Bali, among them many artists and artisans who had formerly been employed at the Majapahit court. This event had a lasting impact on the religious and cultural life of the island and introduced new elements into Balinese temple architecture.

Majapahit Correspondences

The ruined temples of East Java reveal that the religious orientation of the Majapahit era was predominantly Hindu, but with a sizable Buddhist constituency. This same combination of Sivaitic Hinduism and Buddhism occurs in Bali except that the relationship between Hinduism and Buddhism is more syncretic in nature, with Hinduism grabbing the higher ground though itself greatly modified by native Balinese influences. Nevertheless a number of parallels with the Majapahit era can still be drawn. For example, the Balinese continue to cremate their dead and cast their ashes upon the sea. And like the ancient Javanese they also conduct a series of post-mortem rituals to free the soul from the pollution of death.

One major difference between modern Bali and Majapahit Java is the absence of a physical representation of the deity in Bali, except in the case of a few pre-Majapahit-era temples of great antiquity.

Pura Sada Kapal

The Pura Sada at Kapal is the oldest dynastic temple in the former Kingdom of Mengwi and exemplifies the 'Majapahit' style of architecture. The sanctuary was almost completely destroyed by a severe earthquake which rocked Bali in 1917, but was restored by the Archeological Service in 1949-50 in the East Javanese style of the original.

The most important structure inside the temple precincts is a shrine, or *prasada*, dedicated to the royal family of Mengwi's deified ancestors. Behind the *prasada*, standing on a low plinth, there is a curious arrangement of 54 stone seats with three larger ones facing them. The story behind them relates how the cremated remains of one of the rulers of Majapahit were taken down to the sea by 54 of his followers and their three leaders, to be cast to the ocean waves, as still occurs in contemporary Balinese mortuary rites. The ashes, together with a bamboo funerary tower, were placed in a small boat (*kapal*) and the party set out from the shore. Unfortunately, they ended up stranded at sea, but their ill-fated voyage has become immortalised in the serried ranks of stone seats and the *prasada* (which represents the funerary tower) at the Pura Sada Kapal. The nearby village of Kapal is also said to derive its name from this legendary maritime mishap.

Pura Taman Pule,
The Pura Taman Pule, in the village of Mas, some 20 kilometres to the north of Denpasar on the road to Ubud, is historically famous for having been the site of the hermitage of Nirartha.

Niche with statue, Pura Taman Puleh, Mas.

The Nirartha Legacy

The promulgation of Hindu and Buddhist doctrines in Bali is attributed to a number of key historical figures typically Brahman priests from Java and their disciples or descendants. A famous early example is the 11th-century reformer Mpu Kuturan (actually more of a Mahayana Buddhist than Hindu Brahman), but perhaps the most renowned of all is 16th-century Javanese priest Danghyang Dwijendra, otherwise known as Nirartha. Nirartha came to Bali from Kediri in East Java, in 1537, in the aftermath of the collapse of the Majapahit empire. Legend has it that he made the crossing from Java on a leaf of the *keluwih* tree. Upon landing near Negara in the kingdom of Jembrana he sat down to rest under an *ancak* tree—the *ancak* is a relative of the banyan under which the

Buddha famously meditated—and his followers subsequently built a temple on the site, the Pura Ancak, today's Pura Prancak.

The Newly Arrived Magically Powerful High Priest

Nirartha was invited to settle in Mas by a local prince, Mas Wilis, but news of his teachings soon reached the ascendant royal house of Gelgel and an emissary was dispatched to bring the Pedanda Sakti Wauh Ruah or 'Newly Arrived Magically Powerful High Priest', to court.

Once installed at the palace of Gelgel, Nirartha concentrated on matters of ritual practice, especially those connected with marriage, pregnancy, childbirth, death and the post-mortem purification of the soul.

He still found time, however, to embark upon several missionary journeys through Bali, Lombok and Sumbawa. During his travels he founded many temples, while the children of his several marriages, both in Java and in Bali, became the progenitors of important Brahman clans, whose descendants still rank among the most important *Brahmana* families in Bali today.

Nirartha's Temple Building Programme

Between 1546 and 1550 Danghyang Nirartha travelled all over Bali, teaching as he went and founding temples along the way. The famous temple of Tanah Lot, in the former kingdom Tabanan, is one such sanctuary. It is said that on one of Nirartha's journeys round Bali, he chose to sleep at this unusual rocky outcrop on the shores of the King-

dom of Tabanan and later recommended that a temple be built there.

A Passion for *Padmasana*

As well as founding new temples, Danghyang Nirartha also encouraged the building of *padmasana* at many of the existing temples he visited. These he dedicated to Ida Sanghyang Widhi Wasa, the Supreme Being or Ultimate Godhead. The *padmasana* at the Pura Taman Puleh, in Mas (right), rests on top of a stone turtle, representing the mythical earth-supporting chelonian, Bedawang Nala. The two serpents coiled around the latter's body are said to stand for man's earthly needs.

The last *padmasana* to be built by Danghyang Nirartha was at Pura Uluwatu on the western-most tip of the Bukit Peninsula, and it was here that he achieved his apotheosis, or liberation (*moksa*), from the endless cycle of rebirth, to become one with the infinite.

Pura Besakih

A Volcanic Erruption

In 1963, Gunung Agung, literally blew its top in the middle of the month-long celebrations of Eka Dasda Rudra (see right). Although this cataclysmic event caused the destruction of many villages in the vicinity and an enormous loss of life, significantly it did not actually damage Pura Besakih, the lava flow coming to a halt just before it engulfed the place. Naturally the inauspicious conjunction of the rites of Eka Dasda Rudra and the eruption of Gunung Agung was interpreted as the wrath of the gods, who were said to be displeased either by the timing of the festival–this was a period of extreme political tensions which culminated in the abortive communist coup of 1965– or else with the manner in which the rites were conducted. In 1979 the ceremony was held again, this time in much more favourable circumstances which included the presence of President Suharto.

Mountains occupy a special place in Balinese cosmology and there is none more sacred than Gunung Agung, the island's highest peak. Gunung Agung is regarded as the navel of the world and local legend has it that it is actually the summit of Mount Meru brought from India by the God Paramasiwa when Hinduism was first introduced to the island. Pura Besakih, which is situated on the southern slopes of Gunung Agung at an altitude of 900 metres, was at one time the principal place of worship for the royal families of Klungkung, Karangasem and Bangli, but today is regarded as the mother temple for all Bali. Although the Besakih temple complex has very ancient origins, the present structures are of comparatively recent construction with few dating back to before the earthquake of 1917. Nevertheless, despite the many renovations that have taken place over the centuries, Pura Besakih still retains its archaic character—some suppose that it may stand on the site of a prehistoric place of worship belonging to the island's pre-Hindu-Buddhist past.

The Pura Besakih Complex

The Pura Besakih complex is made up of a number of different sanctuaries—there are 22 temples in all—which are situated on parallel ridges running down the mountainside of Gunung Agung. The main temple is the Pura Penataran Agung and it is dedicated to Siwa who occupies the most prominent position in the Balinese pantheon. Pura Batu Madeg, or the 'Temple of the Erect Stone'—a reference to the phallic-shaped monolith that it houses—stands a little to the left (as one faces towards Gunung Agung) and is dedicated to Brahma, the Creator. The Pura Dangin Kreteg, or 'Temple East of the Bridge', is situated on the other side of the main sanctuary, and is dedicated to Vishnu. Together the three deities consitute the Hindu triumvirate, or *trimurti*, but there are also a great many sanctuaries dedicated to other Balinese gods as well as several ancestral temples venerating the deified ancestors of various clans, including, as mentioned earlier, the royal houses of Klungkung, Karangasem and Bangli.

Pura Penataran Agung

Pura Penataran Agung—the Great temple of State—is the symbolic centre of the Besakih complex and comprises six terraces which bare witness to successive enlargements, the most recent being in 1962. There are 57 structures in the temple sanctuary, dedicated to various members of the Balinese pantheon, the principal deity represented here being Siwa. The *meru* towers were probably introduced during the 14th century, possibly in response to Majapahit influences. The lotus throne, or *padmasana*, dates from the 17th or 18th century and acts as the ritual focus of the *pura* and indeed the Besakih complex as a whole.

The Annual Cycle of Festivals

There are more than 70 festivals held regularly at Pura Besakih with almost every shrine in the temple complex celebrating its own anniversary each year. These festive cycles are generally tied to the 210-day *wuku* calendrical system, but the most important ceremonies follow the lunar calendar.

The great annual festival of Bhatara Turun Kabeh (literally, 'The Gods Descend Together') lasts for a whole month and takes place during the tenth lunar month of the year— somewhere between March or April. At this time it is supposed that the gods of all the temples in Bali, great and small, take up residence in the main sanctuary at Pura Besakih and tens of thousands of people from all over the island come to worship at the sacred *padmasana* lotus throne.

Ritual Purification of the Universe

Pura Besakih is also the site of the greatest Balinese ceremony of all—the Eka Dasda Rudra, or Purification of the Universe—which is held once every century. The principal aim of Eka Dasda Rudra is to placate and propitiate Rudra, one of the most ancient of Indian deities, pre-Hindu in his origins, who is associated with disease, plagues, tempestuous winds and other natural disasters. One of the climaxes of the festival is a huge blood sacrifice, which ideally should include every type of creature indigenous to the island—on the last occasion, representatives of some 85 different species were dispatched.

The Focus of Faith

The symbolic centre of the Pura Besakih complex is the lotus throne, or *padmasana*, in the main Pura Penataran Agung sanctuary. Visited by tens of thousands of Balinese during major festivals, this focus of prayer and worship takes the form of a three-seated throne, dedicated to the godhead Ida Sanghyang Widhi Wasa, as manifest in the triple persona of Siwa, Sadasiwa and Paramasiwa, or alternative the Hindu triumvirate of Brahma, Siwa and Vishnu. The view here is from behind, showing the ornately sculpted backs to the three thrones.

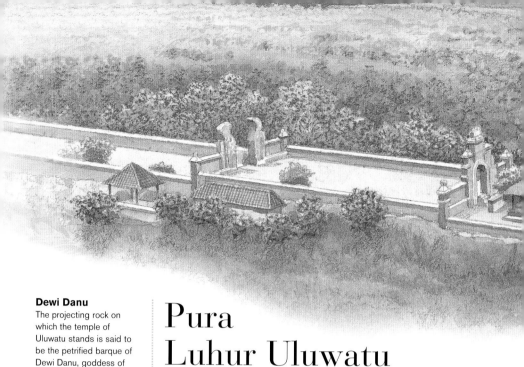

Dewi Danu
The projecting rock on which the temple of Uluwatu stands is said to be the petrified barque of Dewi Danu, goddess of the waters.

Ganesha
Both the inner and outer gateways of Pura Uluwatu are flanked by statues of the elephant god, Ganesha, which is quite unusual in Bali. Ganesha is identified as the remover of obstacles, especially in literary and educational matters and in this last respect he has come to be identified with the acquisition of wisdom.

Pura Luhur Uluwatu

The spectacularly located Pura Luhur Uluwatu, on the westernmost tip of the rocky Bukit Peninsula, is one of the *sad kahyangan*, or 'six great sanctuaries' on the island of Bali. The temple is dedicated to the supreme godhead, Ida Sanghyang Widhi Wasa, in his manifestation as Rudra, the dissolver of life. Violent storms or other cataclysmic interventions of nature such as plagues or volcanic eruptions are said to be Sanghyang Widhi acting in his capacity as Rudra and the location of Pura Uluwatu serves him well.

Historical Associations
Pura Uluwatu is said to have been founded by the Sivaite priest and sage, Mpu Kuturan, who came to Bali from Java in the early years of the 11th century. Though his teachings seemed to have incorporated many Buddhist elements, Mpu Kuturan is said to have been responsible for a revival of Hinduism in Bali at a time when the religion was in decline.

Pura Uluwatu is also associated with the legendary Nirartha who is credited with being the principal architect of a 16th-century Hindu Renaissance in Bali around the time of the collapse of the Majapahit dynasty In East Java. Like Mpu Kuturan, Nirartha founded many temples and encouraged the building of *padmasana* shrines at existing sanctuaries, including the *padmasana* at Pura Uluwatu. It is claimed that it was at Pura Uluwatu that Nirartha achieved his final liberation from the endless cycle of rebirth, becoming one with the godhead. This singular event resulted in the word *luhur* being added to the name of the temple—*luhur* comes from the verb *ngeluhur*, meaning 'to go up', a reference to the apotheosis of Nirartha.

The Temple
Pura Uluwatu is built from dark grey coral stone which is much harder and more durable than the volcanic tuff which is normally used for most Balinese temples. This has meant

that the stone sculptures and decorative elements are better preserved here than in the case of other ancient sites. It is difficult, however, to put a precise date to the existing structures because the temple had been renovated and rebuilt many times in the course of its long history. At the very beginning of this century, part of the temple collapsed into the sea which required substantial reparations, while the most recent restoration work was carried out in the 1980s.

The three *candi bentar* gateways at Pura Uluwatu are unusual in that the upper portions have been sculpted in the shape of wings—the Balinese themselves refer to this type of *candi bentar* as 'winged' (*bersayap*). The oldest of the three *candi bentar*, which leads into the central courtyard, is also incised with stylized flying birds which one scholar has identified as a Balinese "version of the Chinese phoenix". Exotic influences notwithstanding, the principal motif ornamenting all three *candi bentar* and the *kori agung* gateway leading into the inner sanctum, is quintessentially Balinese, namely the head of *bhoma*. Some of these are surmounted by an image of Mount Meru, the cosmic mountain

at the centre of the Hindu-Buddhist universe, while over the *kori agung* gateway, one finds a representation of an urn. The latter is identified as the sacred vessel holding ambrosia (*amrta*), the immortal elixir of life, which in Indian mythology was extracted by the gods from the primeval ocean of milk.

Lightening Strikes

Only those who have come to pray may enter the inner sanctum, but one can get a general view from a terrace on the southern side of the central courtyard. The most important structure in the enclosure is a three-tiered *meru* which stands at the far end. This was struck by lightening a few years back—a very singular and inauspicious event, which could only be redressed by elaborate rites of purification and a rededication of the temple.

Kori Agung

The middle courtyard is dominated by a *kori agung* gateway which leads into the inner sanctum. Its design is very unusual for Bali, being distinguished by an arch or *gapura,* an architectural device which seldom occurs in the Balinese repertoire. The arch has no key stone as such, the apex being completed instead by two large horizontal blocks which perform the function of a lintel. Over the top of the arch there is a leering *bhoma* head to deter malign influences from entering the inner sanctum, and above this stands a sculpture of the *kamandalu,* the sacred vessel which holds the elixir of life.

BIBLIOGRAPHY

Budihardjo, Eko
1986   *Architectural Conservation in Bali.* Gadjah Muda University Press.

Covarrubias, Miguel
1937   *The Island of Bali.* Oxford University Press reprint [1972].

Geertz, Clifford
1973   "Internal Conversion" in Contemporary Bali', in *The Interpretation of Cultures.* New York: Basic Books.

Goris, R.
1960   'The Temple System', in W.F. Wertheim (ed.) *Bali: studies in life, thought and ritual.* The Hague: van Hoeve.

**Hobart, Angela,
Urs Ramseyer
& Albert Leemann**
1996   *The Peoples of Bali.* Oxford: Blackwells Publishers Ltd.

Hobart, Mark
1978   'The Path of the Soul: The legitimacy of Nature in Balinese Conceptions of Space', in G. Milner (ed.) *Natural Symbols in South-East Asia.* London: School of Oriental and African Studies.

1986   'Thinker, Thespian, Soldier, Slave? Assumptions about Human Nature in the Study of Balinese Culture', in Mark Hobart & Robert H. Taylor (eds.) *Context ,Meaning and Power in Southeast Asia.* New York: Ithica, Cornell Southeast Studies Program.

Kempers, Bernet
1991   *Monumental Bali: Introduction to Balinese Archaeology & Guide to the Monuments.* Singapore: Periplus Editions.

Kwa Chong Guan
1995   'Sraddha Sri Rajapatani: an Exploration of Majapahit Mortuary Ritual', in *The Legacy of Majapahit.* Catalogue of an Exhibition at the National Museum Singapore: Singapore National Heritage Board.

Santiko, Hariani
1995   'Early Research on Savaitic Hinduism During the Majapahit Era', in *The Legacy of Majapahit.* Catalogue of an Exhibition at the National Museum Singapore: Singapore National Heritage Board.

Tadgell, Christopher
1990   *The History of Architecture in India.* London: Phaidon Press Ltd.